HOW DO WE

FLYING THROUGH TIME

JOHN COCKCROFT

GENERAL EDITOR: DAVID PENROSE

INTRODUCTION

Flying Through Time is intended for children in the upper junior/lower secondary years of school and considers not only the concept of change as related to aviation but also the evaluation of the evidence at hand.

The book begins with man's earliest desire to fly and concludes with space travel and a view to the future. Interest, curiosity and imagination are stimulated by the many different varieties of source material which the reader is called upon to use and evaluate.

In tracing the development of the flying machine, this book is more concerned with human achievement and the different forms of historical evidence than with technological innovation.

John Cockcroft is the Head of a Junior and Infant school in Leeds. He has many years' teaching experience in Birmingham and Ipswich.

First published in Great Britain 1988 by
Collins Educational
8 Grafton Street, London W1X 3LA

Typeset by Scribe Design, Gillingham, Kent
Printed and bound by Scotprint Ltd, Musselburgh, Scotland

ISBN 0 00 315410 6

CONTENTS

A Greek vase

An Egyptian tomb

Dreams and plans

People have always wanted to fly. For a very long time it was just a dream. People thought their gods could fly. The pictures on the opposite page were made thousands of years ago.

Can you think of any beings or creatures from folk tales or fairy stories who can fly? See how many your class can think of. You could make a wall picture of all of them with their names.

There are many very old stories about flying. One famous tale from ancient Greece is about Icarus and his father Daedalus. To escape from their enemies they stuck feathers to their arms with wax. All went well until Icarus flew too near the sun and the wax melted.

A bronze statue of Icarus made in Greece

If people wanted to fly they needed wings like birds ... or so early fliers thought. So inventors made wings and tried to flap their way into the air. Nobody realised that the human body is not strong enough to fly in this way.

About 400 years ago an Italian artist called Leonardo da Vinci made some better designs for flying machines. There were no motors in those days, but he thought his machines could be worked by levers and pedals.

Look at these pictures drawn by da Vinci. What do you think Leonardo had looked at before he designed his machines?

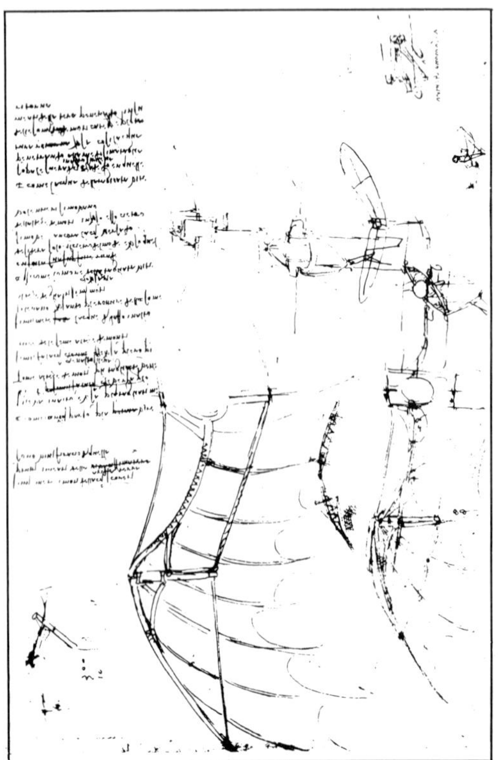

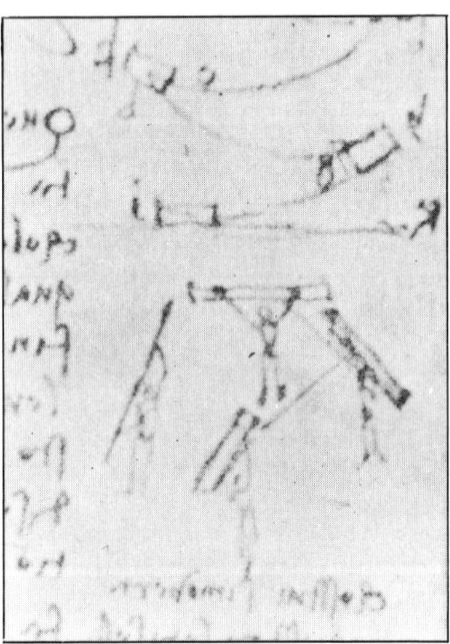

Above left: a design for a fixed wing aircraft
Above right: a design for a simple hang-glider

These designs were probably never made. What do you think would have happened to them if they had been?

First to fly

The first real flight did not happen by copying the birds. Joseph Montgolfier, a French paper manufacturer, wondered why smoke rises. He wondered if it would be possible to lift something by using the rising smoke. He made a small silk bag and burnt some paper inside the open neck. The bag filled with smoke and rose to the ceiling.

Joseph and his brother Etienne began to experiment with balloons and on 21st November 1783 the first manned flight in history took place. The gigantic Montgolfier balloon was made of cloth and crewed by Pilâtre de Rozier and the Marquis d'Arlandes. There was a brazier burning in the mouth of the balloon, and they had to keep the fire going while making sure that the sparks did not set fire to the balloon.

- What do you think the tall posts were used for?
- Why was it necessary to have a brazier burning in the neck of the balloon?
- Why was it to be expected that the balloon might catch fire?
- How could the balloonists control the height at which their balloon flew?
- How would they land their balloon?

The Montgolfier balloon

Ten days after the Montgolfier flight, Charles and Noel Robert went up in a balloon filled with the new 'water gas', or *hydrogen*, which is lighter than air.

Why do you think hydrogen-filled balloons became more popular than those using fires?

What things would you have taken in a balloon?

The balloons went up and came down well enough, but the direction they took depended on the wind. The early *aeronauts* tried steering with oars, sails and propellers. After a lot of experiments people thought that long, cigar-shaped balloons were the easiest to steer. But there was no engine light and powerful enough to move a balloon without the help of the wind.

Giffard's airship

Henri Giffard built a light steam engine to power his *airship* in 1852, but this could only fly in very calm weather. It was not until 1884 that an airship could be steered in any direction regardless of the wind. This was *La France*, which had an electric motor giving it a speed of 23 kilometres per hour.

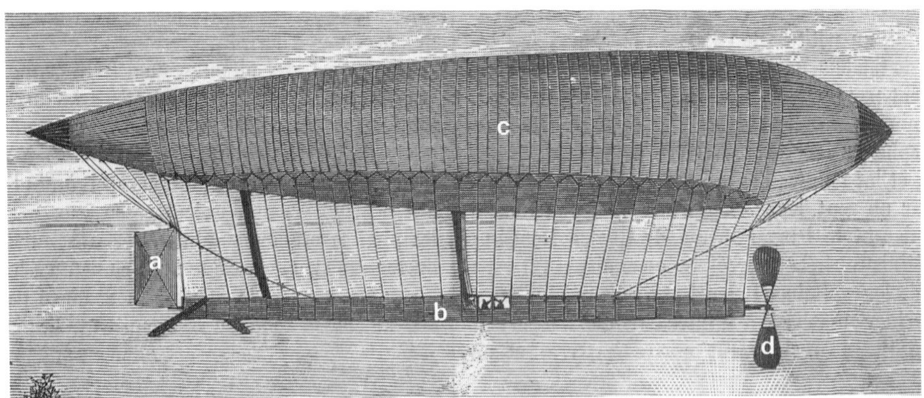

La France

- What are the things labelled a to d?
- How was *La France* more like an aeroplane than a ship?
- What did both balloons use for *lift*?

You can read about how airships developed on page 34.

Heavier-than-air

During the time that lighter-than-air balloons were becoming popular, an Englishman, Sir George Cayley, was working hard to invent a heavier-than-air machine.

Like many an inventor before him, he watched birds flying. But instead of trying to make a machine with flapping wings, he thought of making fixed wings. He would have rudders to control height and direction.

He worked out that the shape of the wing was important to obtain 'lift'. The upper side of the wing had to be curved and the underneath flat. Air passing over the wing had to travel further and so would travel faster than air passing underneath. The air would be spread more thinly on the upper surface of the wing, so the pressure of the air pushing down on it would be lower. The greater air pressure underneath would then 'lift' the whole wing upwards.

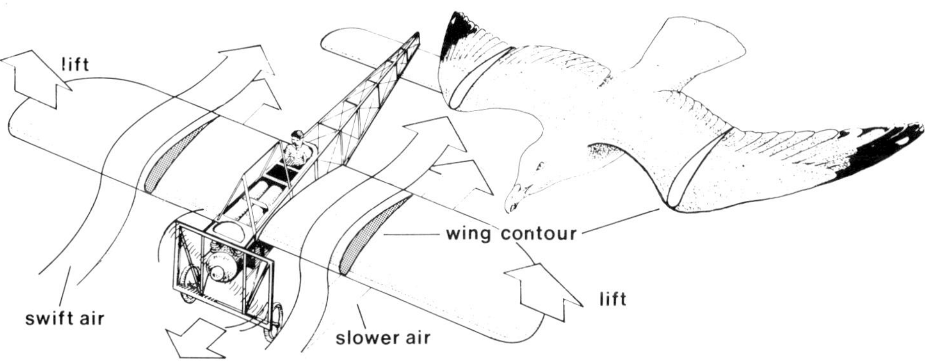

To test the secret of wings, place a strip of paper into a book. Hold the surface of the book up to your mouth, with the strip of paper hanging away from you. Take a deep breath and blow strongly. The wind you make lowers the pressure along the top of the paper and the higher pressure underneath lifts it up.

Cayley developed his ideas by experimenting with gliders which were rather like kites. At first these were models, but in 1850 he built a full-sized glider which was the first heavier-than-air machine to carry a person in free flight.

Here is how Sir George saw the future aeroplane. His words are quite difficult to understand, but you can work it out with a dictionary:

> This is the problem: to provide a plane surface of a given weight, driven by a force strong enough to overcome wind resistance; with wings set at an angle to ensure lateral stability; a rudder for controlling vertical movement and another for direction and powered by engines equipped with propellers.

- Does it sound like a modern aeroplane?

Cayley's ideas had to wait for a long time because there was no engine small enough to provide the power that was needed. But he wrote about his experiments and his work helped other engineers in later years. He published his work in a magazine called *Mechanics' Magazine* which was very popular with people interested in flying.

Here is the front page from one of the issues showing one of Sir George's flying machines.

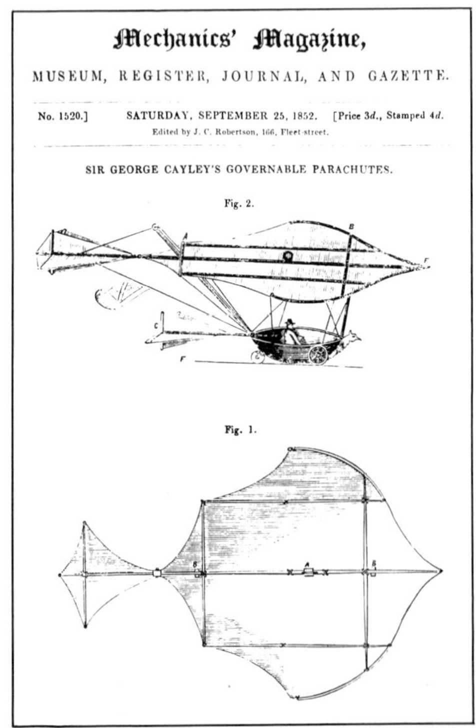

Mechanics' Magazine,

MUSEUM, REGISTER, JOURNAL, AND GAZETTE.

No. 1520.] SATURDAY, SEPTEMBER 25, 1852. [Price 3*d*., Stamped 4*d*.

Edited by J. C. Robertson, 166, Fleet-street.

SIR GEORGE CAYLEY'S GOVERNABLE PARACHUTES.

Fig. 2.

Fig. 1.

- Is it anything like an aeroplane of today?
- In what ways is it similar to a kite?
- Where could you read more about this machine?
- Notice the date on this source. How long ago was it?
- Why do you think he wrote about his work in the *Mechanics' Magazine*?

The hang glider

One of the most famous of the engineers who followed Cayley in later years was Otto Lilienthal, who made more than 2000 glider flights, using both *monoplanes* (single wings) and *biplanes* (double wings). He invented the hang glider. The pilot was held by his arms and controlled the aircraft by swinging his body backwards and forwards. In this way Otto learnt a great deal about controlling an aeroplane.

Here is a photograph of Otto Lilienthal attempting a flight. He lived from 1848 to 1896.

- What does this picture tell you about photography?
- What do we call an aeroplane with two wings?
- What very modern form of flying does the picture remind you of?
- In what ways does this machine look like an aeroplane?
- What power does this machine depend on to stay in the air?
- Where would this flight have had to begin?

Cayley's and Lilienthal's ideas were used by Orville and Wilbur Wright, whom you can read about in the next chapter.

The Wright brothers

The inventors of the first powered machine to fly in any direction chosen by the pilot were two Americans, the brothers Wilbur and Orville Wright. The aeroplane was called *The Flyer*.

Here is part of Orville's diary which describes the first powered flight in 1903. His writing is sometimes hard to read and so we have *transcribed* parts of it.

52

by noon and got the machine out on the tracks in front of the building ready for a trial from the level. The wind was gradually dying and by the time we were ready was blowing only about 4 to 5 meters per. sec. After waiting several hours to see whether it would breeze up again we took the machine in.

Thursday, Dec. 17th

When we got up a wind of between 20 and 25 miles was blowing from the north. We got the machine out early and put out the signal for the men at the station. Before we were quite ready, John T. Daniels, W. S. Dough, A. D. Etheridge, W. C. Brinkley of Manteo, and Johnny Moore of Nags Head arrived. After

53

running the engine and propellers a few minutes to get them in working order, I got on the machine at 10:35 for the first trial. The wind according to our anemometers at this time was blowing a little over 20 miles (corrected) 27 miles according to the Government anemometer at Kitty Hawk. On slipping the rope the machine started off increasing in speed to probably 7 or 8 miles. The machine lifted from the truck just as it was entering on the fourth rail. Mr. Daniels took a picture just as it left the tracks. I found the control of the front rudder quite difficult on account of its being balanced too near the center and thus had a tendency to turn itself when started so that the rudder was turned too far on one side and then too

Thursday, Dec. 17th

When we got up a wind of between 20 and 25 miles was blowing from the north. We got the machine out early and put out the signal for the men at the [life-saving] station. Before we were quite ready, John T. Daniels, W. S. Dough, A. D. Etheridge, W. C. Brinkley of Manteo and Johnny Moore of Nags Head arrived.

After running the engine and propellers a few minutes to get them in working order, I got on the machine at 10.35 for the first trial. The wind according to our anemometer [an instrument measuring speed and direction of wind] at this time was blowing a little over 20 miles [11–12 metres per second] ... 27 miles according to the Government anemometer at Kitty Hawk. On slipping the rope the machine started off increasing in speed to probably 7 or 8 miles. The machine lifted from the track ... Mr Daniels took a picture just as it left the tracks ... A sudden dart when out about 100 feet from the end of the tracks ended the flight. Time about 12 seconds ...

- What made the flight especially difficult?
- How long did this flight last?

This is the photograph which is mentioned in the extract. Pick out Wilbur. Where do you think Orville is?

• What sort of place do you think was chosen to do the flight and why?

You can see a replica of *The Flyer* in the Science Museum in London. In which country would you expect to find the original aeroplane?

At the time of the flight, American newspapers did not know whether to believe the story and of the 22 newspapers to which the story was offered only 5 reported it. Can you think why?

Few foreign newspapers mentioned the story. *The Times* in Britain did not cover it at all. Here is what the *Daily Mirror*, 19 December 1903, reported.

> **THE LATEST AIRSHIP**
>
> According to the "American" (New York), Messrs. Wright Brothers have successfully experimented with a balloonless airship at Kitty Hawk, in Virginia.
>
> The machine, which is really an immense kite with propellers and steering apparatus, is said to have made eight miles an hour against a twenty-one mile wind.

• How does this report differ from the account in Orville Wright's diary?

• Which do you think is the best evidence that this event really took place?

• Using all the sources printed in this chapter, work out exactly where and when this first flight took place.

Louis Blériot

On Sunday, 25 July 1909, Louis Blériot was the first person to fly across the English Channel.

After the Wright Brothers showed the way, people were flying longer and longer distances but there was something special about flying across the English Channel and the *Daily Mail* had offered a prize of £1000 to the first person to do so.

This is how the event was reported in *The Times*, 26 July 1909.

Cross-Channel Flight

The monoplane rose almost immediately, flew half a mile towards Sangette then turned to the right and, passing over the sandhills, crossed the coastline exactly at 4.42 just a hundred yards from where I had taken up the highest position obtainable. Through my telescope I was able to watch the tiny craft long after she had passed from the view of those around me, and after 5 minutes I noticed that she seemed to turn to the left, and proceeded for nearly a mile on a south-east course. After this she again headed for Dover, the height above the sea being I imagine, 250 feet at most ...

Here is part of Blériot's own account of the flight, which was printed in the *Daily Mail*, 26 July 1909.

"MY FLIGHT"

by LOUIS BLERIOT

DOVER, Sunday

At 3.30 a.m. we [Blériot and a friend] went to the garage and examined the aeroplane, which is my eleventh. I started the engine and found that it worked well. All was ready for the start ...

THE HISTORIC AEROPLANE.

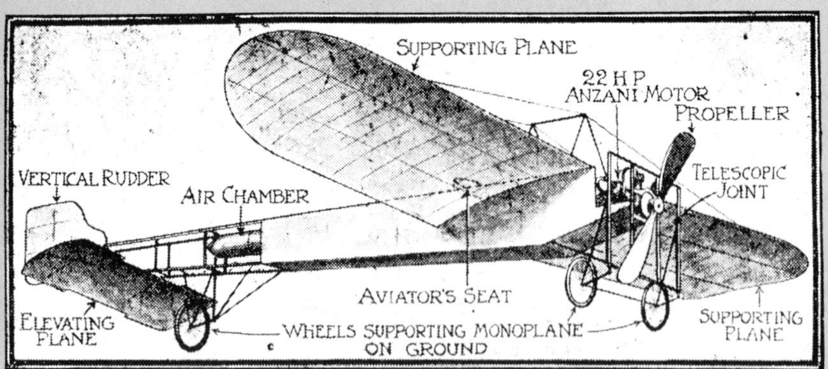

I was dressed as I am at this moment, a "khaki" jacket lined with wool for warmth over my tweed clothes and beneath my engineer's suit of blue cotton overalls. My close-fitting cap was fastened over my head and ears ...

4.35! Le Blanc gives the signal and in an instant I am in the air, my engine making 1,200 revolutions—almost its highest speed—in order that I may get quickly over the telegraph wires along the edge of the cliff. As soon as I am over the cliff I reduce my speed. There is now no need to force my engine.

"I BEGIN."

I begin my flight, steady and sure, towards the coast of England. I have no apprehensions, no sensations ...

Below me is the sea, the surface disturbed by the wind, which is now freshening. The motion of the waves beneath me is not pleasant. I drive on.

LOST!

...I turn my head to see whether I am proceeding in the right direction. I am amazed. There is nothing to be seen ...

For ten minutes I am lost. It is a strange position, to be alone, unguided, without compass, in the air over the middle of the Channel.

...Twenty minutes after I have left the French coast, I see the green cliffs of Dover, the castle, and away to the west the spot where I intended to land.

What can I do? It is evident that the wind has taken me out of my course. I am almost at St. Margaret's Bay and going in the direction of the Goodwin Sands ...

I press the lever with my foot and turn easily towards the west, reversing the direction in which I am travelling. Now, indeed, I am in difficulties, for the wind here by the cliffs is much stronger and my speed is reduced as I fight against it. Yet my beautiful aeroplane responds. Still steadily I fly westwards, hoping to cross the harbour and reach the Shakespeare Cliff. Again the wind blows. I see an opening in the cliff ...

Once more I turn my aeroplane, and, describing a half-circle, I enter the opening and find myself again over dry land ...

At once I stop my motor, and instantly my machine falls straight upon the land from a height of 20 metres (65 feet).

Soldiers in khaki run up, and a police-man ... The conclusion of my flight overwhelms me.

When Blériot saw the English coast, he realised he was on the wrong course. What would have happened if he had continued in that direction?

Look at the diagram of Blériot's aeroplane. What differences can you see between it and the one flown by the Wright brothers?

Below is a memorial to Blériot. It is at a place now named Blériot-Plage, where Blériot began his historic flight.

There are 3 pieces of evidence for Blériot's flight on these pages. Which one do you think is the most important and why?

As you can see in this chapter and the following ones, newspapers are important sources of historical evidence. They are cheap and popular and are published daily. Reporters on-the-spot can describe what actually happened and can collect the memories of witnesses.

Why do you think this book uses a lot of newspaper evidence?

War in the air—1914–1918

After Blériot the design of aeroplanes improved quickly. Blériot's plan for putting the rudders at the back was more effective than the design of the Wright Brothers. French inventors led the way and French words like *fuselage* and *ailerons* were added to the English language.

Flying was still treated as a sport and when the First World War came the generals could see little use for the aeroplane. However, there were some obvious uses as this passage from the autobiography of a First World War pilot, Wing Commander W S Douglas, shows.

> The first time I ever encountered a German machine in the air, both the pilot and myself were completely unarmed. Our machines had not been climbing well, and I was somewhat heavy for an observer, Harvey-Kelly the pilot told me to leave behind all unnecessary gear. I therefore left behind my carbine and ammunition. We were taking photographs of the trench system to the north of Neuve Chapelle when I suddenly espied a German two-seater about 100 yards below us. The German observer did not appear to be shooting at us. There was nothing to be done. We waved a hand to the enemy and proceeded with our task. The enemy did likewise.

- What was the purpose of this flight?
- Why was the crew unarmed?
- Find out what a carbine is. Why did the writer leave his behind?

The aeroplane in the passage was being used for *photo-reconnaissance*. (Look up reconnaissance in your dictionary). On the opposite page is a photograph taken from an aeroplane and a map made from it.

- Who might find such a map useful?
- Make a list from the map of all the details which show that there is a war on.
- What date was the map made?
- Why were aeroplanes good machines for reconnaissance?

Try and find an aerial photograph from your own library of an area near you and draw an *interpretation sketch* from it.

Designers tried to make aeroplanes which could fly higher and faster and which were easier to fly. New ideas which gave one side an advantage were quickly copied by the other side.

INTERPRETATION SKETCH
illustrating natural & topographical features, etc.

"A" Corps I.B.S. No 212. 13·7·18.

Eventually aeroplanes came to have other uses, as this poster from 1915 shows.

- What does the poster warn against?
- What other type of flying machine is shown in the poster?
- Why were British as well as German aeroplanes shown on the Public Warning?

As well as dropping bombs on the enemy, aeroplanes were being fitted with machine guns so that other aeroplanes could be shot down out of the sky. Some pilots became very successful at shooting down aeroplanes, but even successful pilots were sometimes victims.

One of the most famous pilots was the German Baron von Richthofen. Look at these two accounts written by Captain A R Brown about how he shot down the man they called 'the Red Baron'. The first account was written some time after the event while the second is from Brown's *logbook*. All pilots keep logbooks, in which they record briefly what they have done on each flight. You will read about other logbooks later on in this book.

> 'Then I slowly pulled back on the stick and gained a little height—a rule in air warfare. Now ... I raked the whole side of the enemy plane with a burst of machine-gun fire. The pilot turned his head and looked at me. I could see his eyes gleaming behind the big goggles. Then, as the bullets thudded all round him, he slumped in his seat. He had stopped firing. Richthofen was dead. Everything happened in a matter of seconds: it took much less time than it takes to tell it. His plane wobbled, went into a dive, and hit the deck.

> Sopwith BR number 7270. 21 April 1918. Time 10.45 am. Locality 62DQ2. Duty OP. At 10.35 I observed two Albatrosses burst into flames and crash. Dived on large formation of 15–20 Albatrosses and D5 scouts and Fokker triplanes. Two got on my tail and I came out. Went back again and dived on a pure red triplane which was firing on Lieutenant May. I got a long burst into him and he went down vertical and was observed to crash by Lt Mellish and Lt May. I fired on two more but did not get them.

- Why do you think that the two accounts are different?

- Can you think why von Richthofen was nicknamed 'the Red Baron'?

Here are photos of the two types of aeroplane involved in the dogfight. Look carefully at the picture of the Fokker DR1. Why was the machine called a 'triplane'?

Fokker DR1

Sopwith Camel F1

Where might you find more information about aircraft in the First World War? One source of evidence could be memories, which is talked about in another book in this series, *Thanks for the Memory*.

Read this article from a local evening newspaper.

A GERMAN embassy and a Suffolk parish council have combined to commemorate the deaths of 16 German wartime airmen.

The airmen died when their Zeppelin was shot down by a fighter near the village of Eastbridge, near Leiston, in June 1917.

Now Theberton and Eastbridge parish council has combined with the West German embassy in London to replace the old plaque which was erected in Theberton church graveyard in memory of the airmen.

Mr Richard White, chairman of the parish council, said the bodies of the airmen had originally been buried in the graveyard.

When they had been moved to a German wartime grave in Staffordshire, a commemorative plaque had been erected in the graveyard ... which had fallen into disrepair.

The article reminded many people of events which happened many years ago and some wrote in with their memories of the German airships called Zeppelins. Look at the poster on page 20 to find out what a Zeppelin looked like.

Memories of Zeppelin Raids

As you can imagine I have many memories of earlier years in Suffolk but two of the most vivid concern German Zeppelins flying over during the 1914–18 War.

The first dropped its bombs at Hoxne, near Eye, killing some horses belonging to a farmer called Flowerdew that were grazing in a meadow. Some army horses in the vicinity managed to escape.

Then there was the excitement at Theberton, near Southwold, when a Zeppelin crashed after being hit from the air by one of our planes. If I remember right six of the crew were buried underneath the wreckage and six were saved. The pilot jumped from the airship, without a parachute, and died. The dead were buried at Theberton Churchyard, though later their remains were dug up and returned to Germany.

H. GOOCH

Sir,—In reply to the letter "Memories of Zeppelin raid", Mr Gooch is wrong in his details of the bombs that were dropped on Hoxne. They were in fact dropped on Grove Farm, Billingford, farmed by Mr F. Flowerdew. Six horses were destroyed and my father, the late Mr G.S. Flowerdew of Eye, had the one horse that survived.

I still remember the night as a child, my father awaking myself and my brother and sisters to go outside and spend the rest of the night sleeping under a straw sack for safety.

R.A. FLOWERDEW

- Where do the accounts of Mr Gooch and Mr Flowerdew differ?
- How does the letter from Mr Gooch differ from what the newspaper article said happened?

Flights across the Atlantic

Alcock and Brown

The progress made in aeroplane design during the First World War meant that an attempt to fly across a far larger stretch of sea than the Channel could be made.

A prize of £10 000 was offered by the *Daily Mail* for the first non-stop flight across the Atlantic Ocean. Find out how many kilometres the Ocean is at its narrowest points. The winners of the prize were two British men, Captain John Alcock and Lieutenant Arthur Whitten Brown, who flew across on the night of the 14/15 June 1919 in a Vickers Vimy Bomber.

Here is the front page of the *Daily Mirror*, 16 June 1919, showing Alcock and Brown, their aeroplane and a map of their route.

"HOW I FLEW THE ATLANTIC" BY CAPT. ALCOCK

The Daily Mirror

CERTIFIED CIRCULATION LARGER THAN THAT OF ANY OTHER DAILY PICTURE PAPER

No. 4,878 MONDAY, JUNE 16, 1919 [16 PAGES.] One Penny.

BRITAIN'S MAGNIFICENT ATLANTIC AIR TRIUMPH

Here are extracts from Alcock's story as printed in the *Daily Mail*, 16 June 1919.

"A TERRIBLE TRIP"

Machine ice-covered

From Our Special Correspondent Clifden, Sunday

Capt. Alcock described his flight to me in the dining-room of the officers' mess at Clifden, and Lieut. Brown later as we raced back to Galway in my motor-car. He said:

"We started at 5.13 p.m., summertime. The weather reports were very good, and for the first hour the conditions were excellent. We passed Signal Hill at 5.28 …

"At dark we were about 4,000ft. up. We found it very cloudy and misty. We were between two layers of cloud and could see neither sea nor sky …

"We could see nothing. The bank of fog was extremely thick and we began to have a very rough time. The air speed indicator jammed. It stood at 90, and I did not know exactly what I was doing. It jammed through sleet freezing on it, and it smelt smoky. We did some comic 'stunts', then I believe we looped the loop and by accident we did a steep spiral. It was very alarming. We had no sense of horizon. We came down quickly from 4,000ft. until we saw the water very near …

"We climbed up to 11,000 ft. It was hailing and snowing. The machine was covered with ice. That was about 6 o'clock in the morning and it remained like that until an hour before we landed. My radiator shutter and the water temperature indicator were covered with ice for 4 or 5 hours.

"Brown had continually to climb up to chip off the ice with a knife. The air speed indicator was full of frozen particles and gave trouble again. They came on when we got lower, an hour before we landed …

"It was a terrible trip. We never saw a boat and we got no wireless message at all …

"We saw land about 9.15 a.m., when we suddenly discovered the coast. It was great to do that. We congratulated each other. We were very pleased our job was over …

"When still over Clifden village I saw after a few minutes, what I took to be a nice field – a lovely meadow. We came down and made a perfect landing. But it was a bog! The wheels sank axle deep in the field, the Vimy toppled over on her nose."

• What problems did Alcock and Brown have on their flight?

Here are two pages from Brown's logbook which was written during the historic flight.

G.M.T 8.20 C.C 120 Dev ___ Var ___ T.C 13h 52m
Alt ___ Az ___ Lat ___ Long ___
Alt ___ Az ___ Lat ___ Long ___
El.Time ___ Distance by Obs ___ by D.R ___ G.S ___ m.p.h
Track ___ Des.Track ___ Diff ___ Wind ___ m.p.h
T.C ___ Var ___ Dev ___ C.C ___ G.M.T ___
A.S 55 Height 9400 Temp cold
Engines (Port (Stbd Temp 80 / 80 R.P.M 1650 / 1650 Oil 70
Petrol Tank No ___ Turned on at G.M.T ___ Flow ___

Remarks : Still in thick cloud and some snow. Planes covered with ice and aileron hinges frozen

G.M.T 20.20 C.C 160 Dev ___ Var ___ T.C 15h 52m
Alt ___ Az ___ Lat ___ Long ___
Alt ___ Az ___ Lat ___ Long ___
El.Time ___ Distance by Obs ___ by D.R ___ G.S ___ m.p.h
Track ___ Des.Track ___ Diff ___ Wind ___ m.p.h
T.C ___ Var ___ Dev ___ C.C ___ G.M.T ___
A.S 65 Height ~ 400 Temp ___
Engines (Port (Stbd Temp 75 / 76 R.P.M 1720 / 1720 Oil ___
Petrol Tank No ___ Turned on at G.M.T ___ Flow ___

Coast to Coast 15h 57m
Flying time 16h 28m

Remarks : In sight of land

Crossed coast at 8.25 a m civil time. Identified Clifden wireless, & landed at 8.40 a m

Why do you think the writing looks untidy? Look at the pictures of the aeroplane in this section and think about the conditions in which Brown wrote his logbook.

In the second extract from the log, there are some sentences which look quite neat. Find the sentences and think about why this is.

The Vickers Vimy flown by Alcock and Brown

The Vickers Vimy is now in the Science Museum in London. Look at the photo. See how the two engines were fixed only a few feet from the pilot's heads. Can you make out wire elbow guards on either side of the cockpit which prevented the fliers' arms from being cut off by the whirling propellers?

Nowadays, aeroplanes flying long distances have an automatic pilot and the real pilot does not have to fly the plane all the time. But Alcock had to hold the steering column for the entire journey across the Atlantic. Imagine the noise, the wind, the cold, the darkness, the danger. How would you have felt?

A tale has grown up about this flight. Apparently it was so cold that the wings of the aeroplane began to grow heavy with ice. Look at the *Daily Mail* extract. Brown is said to have left his seat and climbed along both wings to hack the ice away from the engines with a knife.

Is there any mention of this in the logbook? Looking at the photo of the aeroplane and, taking into account the ice, the darkness, the speed at which the aeroplane was travelling, think about whether it was possible for a man to do this. How and why might such a story begin? How do you think you might check the truth of the story?

Read this extract from the *Daily Mail*, 16 June 1919. How did the officials from the *Daily Mail* check that the Vickers Vimy had actually flown the Atlantic?

AERO CLUB INSPECTION

Major Mayo representing the Royal Aero Club, accompanied by the Irish Correspondent of the *Daily Mail*, arrived in Galway by aeroplane from Dublin last evening and proceeded to Clifden by motorcar.

Major Mayo inspected the Vickers "Vimy" machine and found the seals and marked parts in order. He also received a letter from the official starter at St. John's.

Which do you think is the most reliable source of evidence in this section?

Charles Lindbergh—the 'Flying Fool'

Alcock and Brown flew across the Atlantic Ocean together. Who would be the first to do it alone?

On Saturday, 21 May, 1927 Charles Lindbergh took off to fly from Long Island, USA, to Paris. These are extracts from his autobiography, *The Spirit of St Louis*, published in 1953.

> Plane ready; engine ready ... the long, narrow runway stretches out ahead. Over the telephone wires at its end lies the Atlantic Ocean; and beyond that, mythical as the rainbow's pot of gold, Europe and Paris.
>
> ... The plane creeps heavily forward. How can I possibly gain flying speed? Why did I ever think that air could carry such a weight? ... The halfway mark is just ahead, and I have nothing like flying speed – the engine's turning faster – smoothing out – the propeller's taking better hold – I can tell by the sound ...
>
> The halfway mark streaks past – seconds now to decide – close the throttle, or will I get off? The wrong decision means a crash – probably in flames – I pull the stick back firmly, and – *The wheels leave the ground.*
>
> I fly through uneasy seconds until Long Island's coast is behind.

This is what the London newspaper, *The Times*, 21 May 1927, said about the take-off:

New York to Paris Flight

Captain Charles Lindbergh alone in his Ryan monoplane, (220hp Wright "Whirlwind"engine) "Spirit of St Louis", left Roosevelt Field, Long Island this morning for a non-stop flight to Paris.

With the supreme disregard for the risk which has characterised all his adventures in the air, he started off with a minimum of preparation. He spent yesterday night sightseeing and returned to the Garden City Hotel at midnight ... At 7.50 a.m. wearing the grin that identified him among the thousands, he crammed his stalwart body into his machine and was off.

His monoplane gathered headway swiftly from its run down the artificial hill ... but it rose only slowly, because of the great weight of petrol it carried.

This is what *The Daily Mirror*, 23 May 1927, said of the flight.

PARIS, Sunday

Clad in a dressing gown he had borrowed from the Ambassador, Captain Lindbergh sat in a room at the United States Embassy yesterday and told his story.

He would not speak much of his own feelings during the flight and once when asked if he felt nervous, replied Lindbergh, "Well I am a fool". This was a joking reference to his nickname – The Flying Fool.

"Before my departure", he said quoted by the Central News, "I had received official reports stating that the atmospheric conditions were excellent. I encountered rain for more than a thousand miles of the crossing. I assure you it was not very pleasant.

"I flew high and I came down low in efforts to find better conditions. Sometimes I was only ten feet above the water, at others, I was ten thousand feet. I never got into really good weather all the way.

"I met no ships during the crossing but during the night I saw the lights of one vessel beneath me. The fact that I saw no more can be easily explained by huge banks of fog."

- Think about the differences in the first two accounts and the reasons for them.

- Do you think that the man who made such a dangerous flight was really a fool? Perhaps you can find reasons from the evidence for your answer.

Now pretend you are a reporter sent to interview Charles in Paris. Make a list of questions you want to ask. Remember that there will be many other people who want to see him. You will not have much time. Keep your questions short and ask only about the most important things.

You might be able to borrow a copy of Charles's autobiography, *The Spirit of St Louis*, from your local library. If they haven't got one, ask for it to be ordered from another library. Then you might be able to find the answers to some of your questions.

Look carefully at the photograph of Charles's plane. Does it look safe for such a long journey? Write a description of it as if you were a newspaper reporter.

Amy Johnson

The air pioneers mentioned so far were all men. But some women flew as well. Some became very famous and made world records of their own, as well as being the first women to fly over routes previously only flown over by men.

One of these women was Amy Johnson, who lived from 1903 to 1941. She set out in May 1930 to break the record for a solo flight from London to Australia.

Amy's flight to Australia was recorded in her logbook or Record of Flights. Here is a page from Amy's Record together with a transcription of the Record of the whole flight.

RECORD OF FLIGHTS.

Date.	Aircraft. Type.	Aircraft. Markings.	Pilot.	Journey.	Time in Air. Hrs.	Time in Air. Mins.	Remarks.
				Brought forward...	99	25	
May 5	Moth	G-AAAH	Self	Croydon to Vienna	07	30	1st stage journey to Australia
" 6	"	"	"	Vienna to San Stefano	10	00	2nd " " "
" 7	"	"	"	San Stefano to Aleppo	05	30	3rd " (petrol leak – ran into clouds in Taurus mountains).
" 8	"	"	"	Aleppo to Baghdad W.	09	15	4th " (dust storm – broke strut).
" 9	"	"	"	Baghdad W. to Bandar Abbas	10	00	5th " (broke strut bolt).
" 10	"	"	"	Bandar Abbas to Karachi	09	45	6th " (engine overhauled).
" 11	"	"	"	Karachi to Jhansi	11	15	7th " (head wind – couldn't reach Allahabad).
" 12	"	"	"	Jhansi to Allahabad	02	00	8th " (refuelled & breakfasted).
				Carried forward...	164	40	

Date	Journey	Time in Air Hrs	Mins	Remarks
May 5	Croydon to Vienna	07	30	1st stage journey to Australia
May 6	Vienna to San Stefano [Istanbul]	10	00	2nd stage journey to Australia
May 7	San Stefano [Istanbul] to Aleppo [Halab]	05	30	3rd stage (petrol leak – ran into clouds in Taurus mountains).
May 8	Aleppo to Baghdad W.	09	15	4th stage (dust storm – broke strut).
May 9	Baghdad W. to Bandar Abbas	10	00	5th stage (broke strut bolt).
May 10	Bandar Abbas to Karachi	09	45	6th stage (engine overhauled).
May 11	Karachi to Jhansi	11	15	7th stage (head wind – couldn't reach Allahabad).
May 12	Jhansi to Allahabad	02	00	8th stage (refuelled and breakfasted).
May 12	Allahabad to Calcutta	08	15	8th stage (headwind).

- Draw a simple map of the world and using the information from her logbook plot her route from London to Darwin, Australia showing the stopping-off places and dates.
- Make a list of the problems she faced with the dates on which she mentioned them.
- Make a block graph of hours flown each day. How many hours did the whole trip take? How long does it take now to fly to Australia?

On 8 May, Amy flew from Aleppo (Halab) to Baghdad. Find details of this flight in her logbook, and find the places on your map.

- How long did this flight take?
- What problems did Amy have on the journey?

RECORD OF FLIGHTS.

Date.	Aircraft.		Pilot.	Journey.	Time in Air.		Remarks.
	Type.	Markings.			Hrs.	Mins.	
				Brought forward...	164	40	
May 12	Moth	G-AAAH	Self.	Allahabad to Calcutta	08	15	8th stage (headwind)
" 13	"	"	"	Calcutta to Rangoon	10	15	9th " (met monsoon) landed at Insein & crashed machine (delayed 2 days) towed to Rangoon race-course
" 16	"	"	"	Rangoon to Bangkok	08	30	10th " (monsoon)
" 17	"	"	"	Bangkok to Singora	06	00	11th " (" headwind)
" 18	"	"	"	Singora to Singapore	10	15	12th " (do)
" 19	"	"	"	Singapore to Tjomal	10	00	13th " (forced landed due to petrol leak headwind)
" 20	"	"	"	Tjomal to Semarang	03	15	14th " (to refuel).
				Carried forward...	221	10	

May 13	Calcutta to Rangoon	10	15	9th stage (met monsoon). Landed at Insein and crashed machine (delayed two days) towed to Rangoon race-course.
May 16	Rangoon to Bangkok	08	30	10th stage (monsoon).
May 17	Bangkok to Singora [on northern peninsula of Malaysia]	06	00	11th stage (monsoon and headwind).
May 18	Singora to Singapore	10	15	12 th stage (monsoon and headwind).
May 19	Singapore to Tyomal [Java]	10	00	13th stage (forced landed due to petrol leak and headwind).
May 20	Tyomal to Semarang	03	15	14th stage (to refuel)
May 20	Semarang to Surabaya	03	00	14th stage (folld. Dutch pilot held up one day).
May 22	Surabaya to Atamboea [on island of Timor]	11	30	15th stage (forced landing at ? – delayed a day).
May 24	Atamboea to Port Darwin	07	00	16th stage (16 days in the air).

Here is Amy's own recollection of this episode in her journey.

> "All went well until I was almost within sight of Baghdad ... Immediately ahead of me appeared a much thicker haze than any I had already encountered and I began to wonder whether it would be too thick for me to see through. Suddenly my machine gave a terrific lurch, the nose dipped, and *Jason* and I dropped a couple of thousand feet .....
>
> In less time than it takes to tell I had dropped to within a few feet from the ground, and was helplessly being blown hither and thither at the mercy of some force I could not understand ... Sand and dust covered my goggles, my eyes smarted, and I couldn't control the machine sufficiently to keep it straight ... I had never been so frightened in my life ... All at once I felt my wheels touch ground although I could see nothing ... The machine swayed and bumped and every second I expected to see it turn over or run into some obstacle. To my untold relief it finally came to rest and I switched off the engine and jumped out as quickly as I could, hindered as I was by my parachute ..."

This extract has the excitement and detail which cannot be found in the logbook. However, read the following extract from a biography of Amy Johnson by Constance Babington Smith, published in 1967. Would you still trust Amy's description?

> Some of the true facts about the flight will probably never be established. Her log book gives only the barest outline of her progress ... Even in her two lectures there are many discrepancies [differences]; she was habitually [often] careless about figures, dates and details of facts ... She herself probably put the lectures together but much of it is indirectly the work of journalists ... Nevertheless, with the help of surviving cables, letters, photographs and contemporary press reports, it is possible to follow the course of the flight more or less accurately.

- What is the difference between a biography and an autobiography?
- How did Amy Johnson's character make writing her biography difficult?
- Do you think the author had actually spoken to Amy? (Clue: compare the dates when Amy died and when the book was published.)
- What sources did Constance Babington Smith make use of?

Choose a famous person who was alive this century but is now dead. Pretend that you are going to write a biography of this person. What different sources of evidence would be of use to you in writing the biography?

Amy Johnson

Airships

The German Zeppelins (see pages 20–23) had proved a frightening weapon in the First World War and encouraged governments to look into the building of a fleet of airships.

Once some people thought airships would be more important than aeroplanes. Many people felt that they would be the only vehicles in which to cross the Atlantic, in luxury, by air. You can now only occasionally see modern airships. They are mainly used by advertising companies to advertise their products.

The following stories will give you the reason why they fell in popularity.

The R101

In 1924 the British government began an airship programme. Two airships were to be built. The R100 was to be built by a private firm and the R101 was to be built at the government aircraft factory. They were to be used to carry large loads and also for long flights around the world.

Here are extracts from a book called *Airships and Balloons* by Carey Fisher, published in 1973.

Plans were now being set in motion for two long and impressive maiden flights for the finished airships. The R100 was to fly to Canada and the R101 to India. The Air Ministry announced that their own ship would be taking the new Indian Viceroy Lord Thomson, to see his new empire in September 1930 ...

There was only time for the one test flight for what was really a brand-new, untried airship... A 'temporary' Certificate of Airworthiness was handed over to the captain as the ship was being loaded. It had been decided, they said, that trials could be carried out with the passengers on board! An amazing gamble when people's lives were at stake.

Effort and expense had been poured into making the interior of the R101 as luxurious as possible. The item which caused the crew the most unease was the arrival of a pale-blue Axminster carpet which not only covered a lounge the size of a tennis court but also a 600 foot long corridor running almost the length of the airship ... The weight of a carpet that size would make a big difference to their precious useful 'lift'!...

The great moment had arrived – the vast dirigible [airship] pulled her nose away from the masthead cone and carefully backed away from it. Her bow instead of soaring upwards as it should have done, dipped slightly and water ballast had to be dropped to prevent the great ship drifting even farther towards the ground—a gloomy portent! [sign]

It was a rough evening and the R101 only managed to travel at one-third of her expected speed. The rain ... pounded unceasingly on the hull of the R101 as she reluctantly made her way towards the coast.

One of the after engines had now failed completely. Her height had dropped to a dangerous 700 feet ... It took three hours to repair the faulty engine, a difficult task for Harry Leech, the engineer, whilst the airship was still in flight.

After leaving the sea, a fierce headwind met the R101 and slowed her already slow progress down to a crawl...

The R101 had passed over the French town of Beauvais and many of the sleeping residents had been awakened by the growl of the overworked engines struggling through the rain. Many of them rushed to their windows and saw the last of the R101 as she glided slowly and gracefully into a hill and exploded.

Here is a report from the *Daily Mirror*, 6 October 1930, about the same event.

THE TRAGIC END OF R101

Survivor's Graphic Story of Disaster

Graphic details of the disaster to R101 were given last night by one of the survivors, Mr Leech, the foreman engineer ...

"We started from Cardington in fine weather but it deteriorated as we approached the Channel, and over the sea it was really bad.

"Nevertheless, the voyage was uneventful until we reached Beauvais, by which time conditions were very rough, the wind and rain being terrific.

"It was not a storm which would normally have given us cause for anxiety, but that spot beyond Beauvais has a bad reputation for air accidents.

"I think it must be the result of eddies [small whirlwinds] caused by the range of hills at that place ...

"Just after passing over Beauvais the ship was weathering the storm well, and the engines were running quite normally when, without warning, she dipped her nose at an angle of 45deg. to the ground.

"She descended some distance, straightened out, then dipped again at the same angle, striking the side of the hill with a terrific crash.

"The forward engine-cars were crushed under the hull, which in turn collapsed and buried the cabins in wreckage. About a second elapsed between the crash and the explosion, which was followed by a roar of flame, and the hull burned from end to end.

"My idea is that the explosion was due to the breakage of electric wires."

- Who was Mr Leech? Notice that Mr Leech says in the newspaper extract that 'the voyage was uneventful until we reached Beauvais.' Look at the description in the book. Does Carey Fisher make the first part of the flight seem uneventful?
- Which of the accounts is 'first-hand' evidence?
- Find any *opinions* as opposed to straight facts in Carey Fisher's account.
- Which of the two accounts of the crash is likely to be the most reliable?

The Hindenburg

In spite of the crash of the R101, other countries, especially Germany, were still interested in airships and wanted to prove that airships were suitable for long flights.

One German, Dr Hugo Eckener, was head of the Zeppelin Company which built many large, luxurious airships which travelled all over the world. The largest and most luxurious was called the *Hindenburg*. It was 245 metres long. Compare this with the largest aeroplane, the Boeing 747, which is 70 metres long.

Eckener wanted to use helium gas in the *Hindenburg*'s airbags rather than hydrogen which had been used in the R101. Unlike helium, hydrogen is *inflammable*, that is it can easily catch fire. At that time, however, only America had helium and they would not sell it to Germany in case they used it for military airships.

By 1937 the *Hindenburg* had been operating for a year and had carried 1200 passengers from Europe to America. On Thursday 6 May 1937, a newscaster for an American radio station, Herb Morrison, was sent to Lakehurst, a place near New York, to report on the first arrival in the 1937 season of the *Hindenburg*. This is a *transcription* of part of his broadcast:

> "It's crashing! It's crashing! Terrible ... it's burning, bursting into flames and ... it's falling on the mooring pad ... this is one of the worst catastrophes in the world ... It's twenty, forty, oh, four or five hundred feet into the sky and it's a terrific great flame, ladies and gentlemen ... Oh, the humanity ... I can't talk, ladies and gentlemen, honest, it's just laying there, a mass of smoking wreckage ... I'm going to have to stop for a minute because I've lost my voice ... Oh this is the worst thing I've ever witnessed!"

A newspaper picture of the Hindenburg in flames

Due to the time difference between America and Britain, the first reports of the crash were in Friday's newspapers. Here is what the *Daily Mail*, 7 May 1937, reported:

ZEPPELIN EXPLODES: 100 DEAD

With 100 passengers and crew on board, the giant Zeppelin Hindenburg, the world's biggest airship, burst into flames as she prepared to moor here this evening at the end of her first flight of the season over the Atlantic.

All the occupants except three are believed to have been killed.

The airship had tossed her nose-lines towards the ground, when suddenly there was a terrific burst of flame from the stern and an explosion that shook the entire district. She crashed and fell from a height of 400 feet, her steel frame becoming a mass of wreckage.

Now read the report in the *Daily Mirror*, the following day, 8 May 1937:

ZEPP CRASH

CAPTAIN Lehmann, who was acting in an advisory capacity to the commanding officer, Captain Max Preuss, died shortly after 6 o'clock this evening, bringing the death roll up to thirty-three ...

All resources are being used to sift possibilities that the wrecking of the Hindenburg was caused by sabotage. The general opinion held here is that hydrogen was ignited by a spark from reversing Diesel motors.

Herr Luther [German Ambassador] declared today: "I am satisfied there was no technical mistake" ...

Dr. Eckener said last night: "I believe in the possibility of sabotage, because on every trip to the United States, particularly when the German air liner visited the Chicago Exhibition, we received many threatening letters."

He added that there was a possibility that a shot had been fired at the dirigible.

Total survivors of the disaster number sixty-four.

- Why do you think that there is a difference between the two papers in the number of deaths reported?
- What reasons does the *Daily Mirror* give for the airship crash?
- Which of these pieces of evidence on the *Hindenburg* would you consider to be the most reliable?

The Battle of Britain

When war broke out again in 1939 people were very worried. They could remember the Zeppelin raids from the First World War and they had seen on newsreels how Germany's modern air force had bombed towns and cities in Spain during the civil war there. A big campaign to build more aeroplanes began and people practised what they would do in an air-raid.

In the summer of 1940 the first ever battle between aeroplanes alone took place called 'The Battle of Britain'. Germany sent squadrons of bombers and fighters over south-east England to try to weaken Britain. They were met by Spitfires and Hurricanes of the Royal Air Force which defeated the German planes even though they were outnumbered.

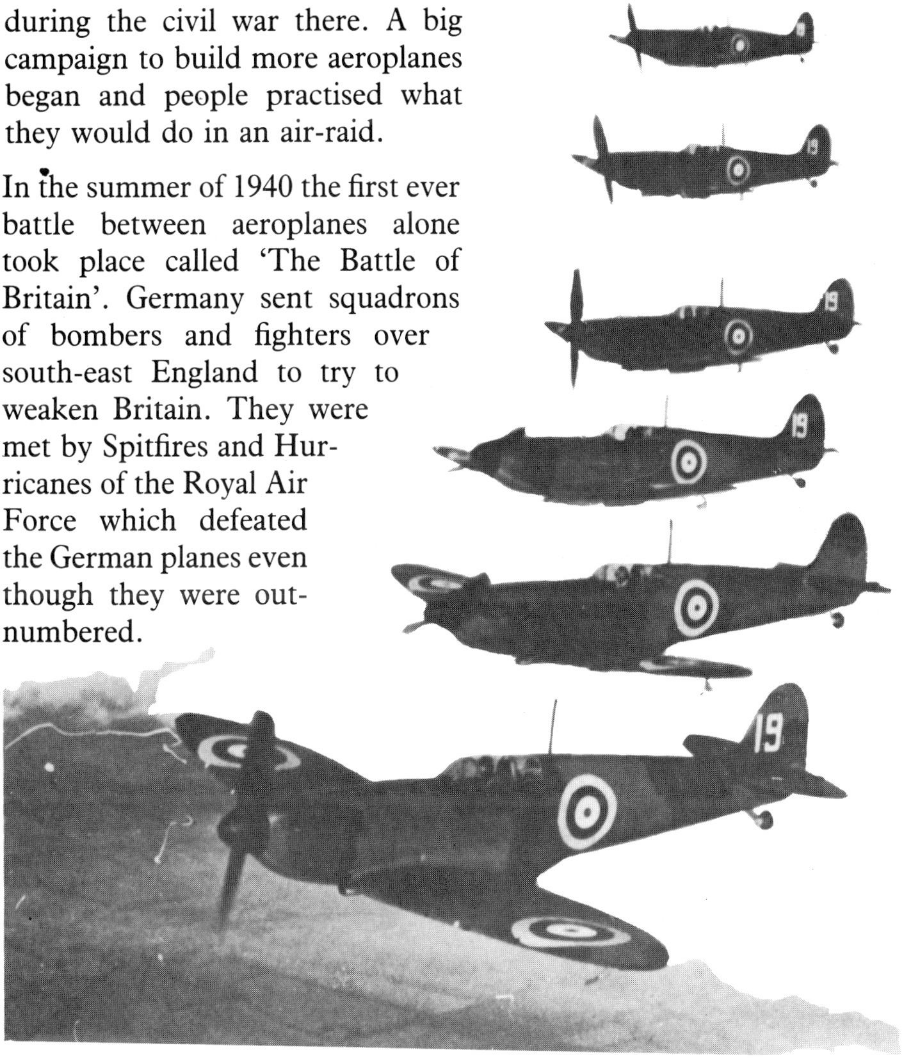

British Spitfires in formation during the Battle of Britain

The British newspapers gave daily records of events throughout the battle, though their accounts were not always accurate. The information they were given about aircraft shot down and aircraft lost was deliberately wrong sometimes. Why do you think this was?

Look at this newspaper article from the *Daily Mirror*, 16 August 1940.

144 DOWN OUT OF 1,000

A HUNDRED AND FORTY-FOUR ENEMY RAIDERS WERE BROUGHT DOWN UP TO MID-NIGHT YESTERDAY.

That was Britain's answer at the end of the day of the greatest air attacks of the war, in which the German "blitz" swept the length of Britain.

Twenty-seven R.A.F. fighters were lost in the mighty defence battles, but eight of the pilots are safe.

For hour after hour through the day, and then into the night, our fighters swept against the huge raiding squadrons.

The German Air Force used more than a thousand bombers and fighters in the attacks.

Croydon Aerodrome, London's air-port before the war, was raided last night. "Bombs were dropped on and around the aerodrome," said the Air Ministry later. "Some damage was done, but details are not yet available."

Sirens were sounded in a wide area of Greater London.

Many towns were attacked during the day, and a number of people killed. R.A.F. aerodromes in the south-east and in the north-east were bombed...

It was the most gruelling day for the R.A.F. fighters. And their greatest.

- How many German aeroplanes are said to have been shot down?
- How many British planes were lost?
- How many people were killed in German raids? Why do you think there are no figures?
- What is a 'blitz'?
- Why were RAF aerodromes attacked? Do you think this piece of news should have had more space?

The table below, drawn up after the war, shows as accurately as possible the actual losses of the German Luftwaffe (air force) on various days of the Battle. It also shows the RAF estimate at the time of planes shot down and the number of planes which the Germans at the time admitted they had lost.

The Battle of Britain

German aircraft destroyed over Britain during the Battle

Date	RAF estimate	German estimate	Actual losses
15 August	183	32	86
18 August	155	36	71
31 August	94	32	39
2 September	66	23	34
7 September	100	26	40
15 September	185	43	56
27 September	153	38	55
Total losses July–October 1940	2692	896	1733

- Why do you think the RAF estimate was too high?
- Why do you think the total admitted lost by the Germans was too low?
- Look at the figures for the 15th August. How do these figures differ from those mentioned in the following day's newspaper (see page 40). Can you think of any reasons why?

More accurate information was recorded by the pilots themselves in their *combat reports*, but these were secret. On the next page is a combat report by Flying Officer Malan.

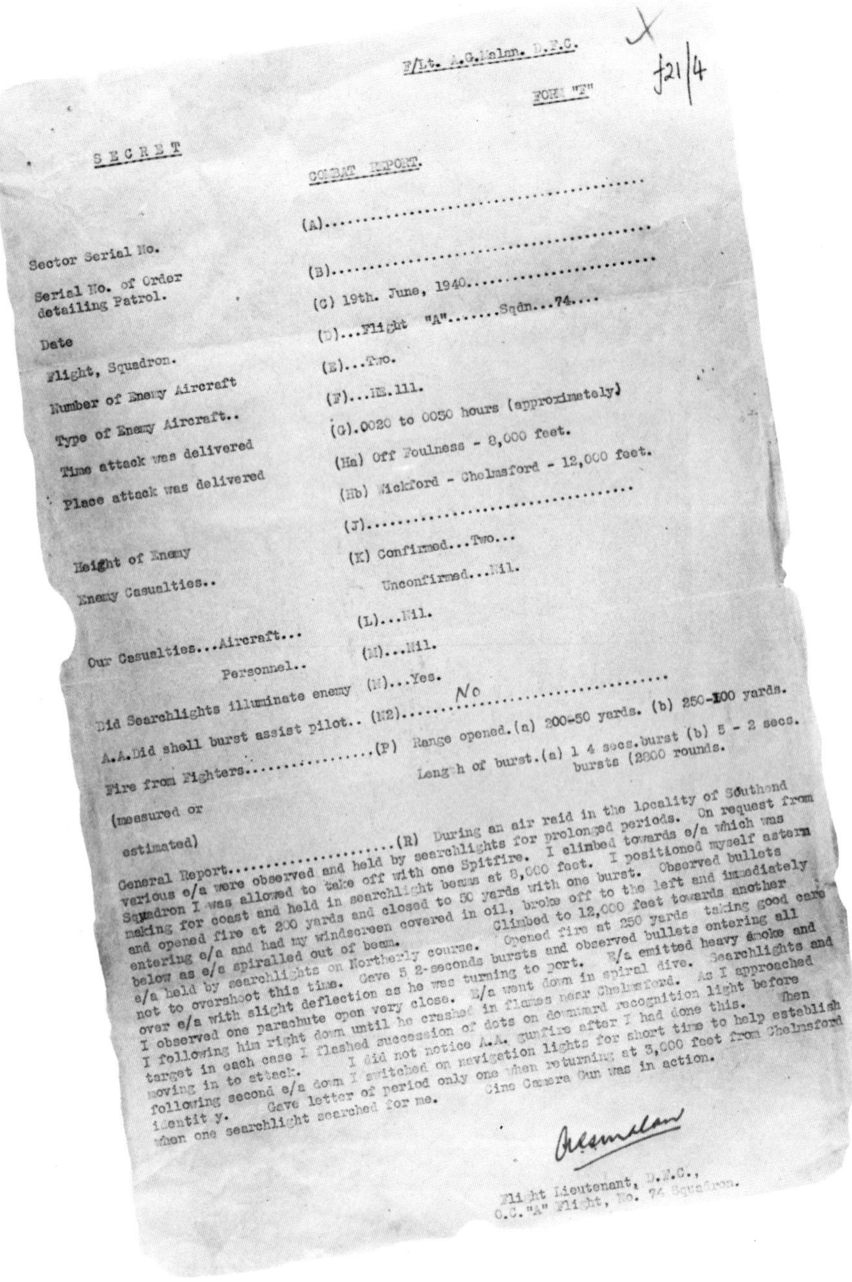

F/Lt. A.G. Malan. D.F.C.

FORM "F"

f21/4

SECRET

COMBAT REPORT.

Sector Serial No. (A)..

Serial No. of Order detailing Patrol. (B)..

Date (C) 19th. June, 1940..............................

Flight, Squadron. (D)...Flight "A".......Sqdn...74....

Number of Enemy Aircraft (E)...Two.

Type of Enemy Aircraft.. (F)...HE.111.

Time attack was delivered (G).0020 to 0050 hours (approximately)

Place attack was delivered (Ha) Off Foulness - 8,000 feet.

(Hb) Wickford - Chelmsford - 12,000 feet.

Height of Enemy (J)..

Enemy Casualties.. (K) Confirmed...Two...

Unconfirmed...Nil.

Our Casualties...Aircraft... (L)...Nil.

Personnel.. (M)...Nil.

Did Searchlights illuminate enemy (N)...Yes.

A.A.Did shell burst assist pilot.. (N2)...No.......................................

Fire from Fighters...............(P) Range opened.(a) 200-50 yards. (b) 250-100 yards.

(measured or estimated) Length of burst.(a) 1 4 secs.burst (b) 5 - 2 secs. bursts (2800 rounds.

General Report.....................(R) During an air raid in the locality of Southend various e/a were observed and held by searchlights for prolonged periods. On request from Squadron I was allowed to take off with one Spitfire. I climbed towards e/a which was making for coast and held in searchlight beams at 8,000 feet. I positioned myself astern and opened fire at 200 yards and closed to 50 yards with one burst. Observed bullets entering e/a and had my windscreen covered in oil, broke off to the left and immediately below as e/a spiralled out of beam. Climbed to 12,000 feet towards another e/a held by searchlights on Northerly course. Opened fire at 250 yards taking good care not to overshoot this time. Gave 5 2-seconds bursts and observed bullets entering all over e/a with slight deflection as he was turning to port. E/a emitted heavy smoke and I observed one parachute open very close. E/a went down in spiral dive. Searchlights and I following him right down until he crashed in flames near Chelmsford. As I approached target in each case I flashed succession of dots on downward recognition light before moving in to attack. I did not notice A.A. gunfire after I had done this. When following second e/a down I switched on navigation lights for short time to help establish identit y. Gave letter of period only one when returning at 3,000 feet from Chelmsford when one searchlight searched for me. Cine Camera Gun was in action.

AGMalan

Flight Lieutenant, D.F.C.,
O.C."A" Flight, No. 74 Squadron.

- What do you think E/a stands for?
- How many enemy aircraft were brought down in the attack?
- What aeroplane was Malan flying?
- Pretend you are a newspaper reporter during the war. Write a report on this attack using the facts in the combat report.

Other evidence of German and British losses can be found in cemeteries in southern England.

Look at these gravestones from the Luftwaffe cemetery in Brookwood in Surrey. Notice the date of death. Work out how old these men were when they died.

When a soldier dies it is usual for his commanding officer to return his personal belongings to his family with a letter. What would such a letter talk about? Write one for one of these airmen.

Women also took part in the air battle. They were members of the WAAF (Women's Auxiliary Air Force), and their job was to listen to reports from the radar operators and guide the British squadrons to meet the enemy.

Look at this photograph of the WAAF at work. Can you see what is happening?

Today, aeroplanes used in the Battle of Britain can be seen in museums like the RAF museum in Hendon or the Imperial War Museum in London. On the opposite page are some photographs taken during the war of the most famous aeroplanes and also pictures of aeroplanes which you can see in museums.

Try to find out which are fighters and which are bombers.

Spitfire

Mosquito

Lancaster

Wellington

Hurricane

Messerschmitt

The struggle for control of the air during the war caused developments in flying which would have taken many years in peacetime. Flying the Atlantic became a safe and common event as more powerful machines with four engines flew higher and faster. Radar allowed 'blind flying' and aeroplanes became more independent of the weather. The jet engine was introduced.

Passenger flying

Before the First World War aeroplanes were not reliable enough for ordinary passenger flights. The war caused a race to improve aeroplanes. In many countries airlines began flights between cities, using converted warplanes. New aeroplanes were designed which were better for passengers and cargo. Mail was sent by air and countries began to issue air mail stamps.

An Australian airmail stamp

There was a lot of competition between airlines and aeroplane makers. This led to aeroplanes which were 1) more comfortable, 2) had more space, 3) were quicker and 4) safer. As a result airlines developed quickly. On ocean routes the airlines used *seaplanes*. Here are some photos of some of the important makes of aeroplane in the development of passenger flight. Look at them closely and see how they have developed.

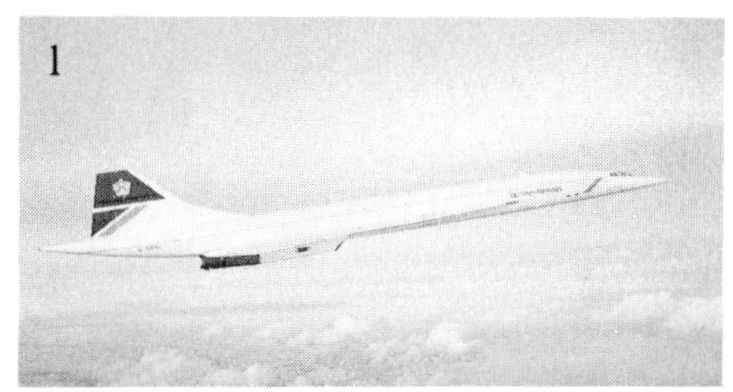

a) Vickers Vimy, early 1920s. Developed from Alcock and Brown's plane.
b) Inside an Armstrong Whitworth Argosy used in the late 1920s.
c) Passengers boarding a Handley Page 42 introduced in the 1930s.
d) Imperial Airways flying boat in use in the 1930s.
e) Douglas DC3 in use in the late 1930s and 1940s. The most widely used and probably the most famous of all airliners.
f) Vickers Viscount introduced in the 1950s. Used turbo engines.
g) De Havilland Comet I, early 1950s. The world's first jet airliner.
h) Lockheed Super Constellation used on the first London to New York service.
i) Bristol Britannia used in the late 1950s.
j) Boeing 707 which began flights in the late 1950s.
k) Boeing 747, also known as the 'Jumbo Jet', made its first flight in 1969 and is the world's largest airliner.
l) Concorde, the first supersonic airliner, began flights in the 1970s.

Look at the chart below which lists various *statistics* for many of the aircraft illustrated. A new machine is not always more advanced than an older one. It takes a long time to design and build an aeroplane. Different manufacturers had different ideas about their machines.

First flight	Aircraft	Weight lbs	Number of engines	Number of passengers	Cruising speed km/h	Range kms
1919	Vickers Vimy Commercial	12500	2	2	151	724
1925	Fokker FVII/3M	11684	3	10	177	1200
1926	Armstrong Whitworth Argosy	19200	3	28	152	836
1930	Handley Page 42	28000	4	28	152	804
1934	Douglas DC2	18560	2	14	318	1609
1949	De Havilland Comet	115000	4	44	788	3218
1950	Lockheed Super Constellation	137000	4	99	571	7434
1952	Bristol Britannia	155000	4	139	539	6115
1969	Boeing 747	775000	4	496	938	8851
1969	BAC Concorde	408000	4	100	2179	6582
1972	Airbus A300	365750	2	375	885	7885

- What is meant by *range*?
- What other things might aeroplane-makers be interested in? Remember the four features mentioned on page 46.
- Can you see any *trends* in the statistics? Start at the top and work down each column. What is happening?
- What can you say about the development of engines and the number of passengers carried?
- Make graphs about the weight, number of passengers, speed and range for a) all the 2-engined airliners, b) for all the 4-engined airliners.
- Why don't all modern aircraft fly as fast as Concorde? If you don't know, get together and decide how you can find out. (Who could you ask? Who could you write to? Where could you find a book?)
- Why is weight important in aircraft design? What things add to the weight of an aeroplane?

Croydon Airport

Look at this advertisement for flights to Paris about 60 years ago, in the late 1920s.

- How long did the flight take?
- When did each flight leave London and arrive in France?
- How many flights a day went to Paris?
- How did Imperial Airways ensure that the flight was safe and reliable as well as comfortable?

Now look at this modern timetable showing British Airways flights.

London to Paris daily

Dep London	Arr Paris	Dep London	Arr Paris
0630	0730	1430	1530
0830	0930	1630	1730
1030	1130	1830	1930
1230	1330	2030	2130

- How long does a flight to Paris take today?
- How many flights does this airline have to Paris every day?

The Silver Wing flight to Paris took off from Croydon Airport in London. Here is a photograph showing the airport at the time.

- Where is the control tower? Can you see the entrance to the airport?
- How could you work out roughly when the photograph was taken?

Here is what Croydon control tower and airport buildings look like now. They are used as offices. What has happened to the airport? Can you think of reasons why this has happened? Think about the other airports now in the area.

Heathrow Airport

Today's flights to Paris from London usually take off from Heathrow. Here is a photograph of Terminal 4 at Heathrow.

- What is the most obvious difference between Heathrow and Croydon Airport?
- What do you think is being loaded onto the aeroplanes before the passengers board?

Here is what Heathrow looked like in 1947. How long ago was that?

- Why do you think it has grown?
- What problems do you think that building an airport might make for:
  - –local residents?
  - –farmers?
  - –conservationists?
  - –the local railways and buses?
  - –the builders?

Today there are so many aeroplanes that they must travel along air routes or 'corridors' in the sky. The earth is divided into regions controlled by air traffic control centres which use radar to keep track of every aeroplane in the sky.

- What help did the early airline pilots have to help them navigate from place to place?
- What help do modern pilots have?
- What had the early airline pilots to fear from the weather? Look at the newspaper accounts of Alcock and Brown, and Lindbergh on pages 24–29.
- What problems does the weather cause modern pilots?

Helicopters

As you have learnt, the first inventors of flying machines watched the birds. Some birds make a running take-off, others use their wings to take off almost vertically.

Air moving over a machine with fixed wings 'lifts' it up into the air. But there is another way. If you can make the wings move fast enough, they can make enough lift to raise the machine straight up into the air.

This idea has been known for a long time. The word helicopter comes from the Greek word for 'spiral', *helix*. Leonardo da Vinci thought that a spiral might be used for flight. Here is a drawing he made of such a machine in about 1490 and a model which has been made, following da Vinci's drawing, by the Science Museum in London.

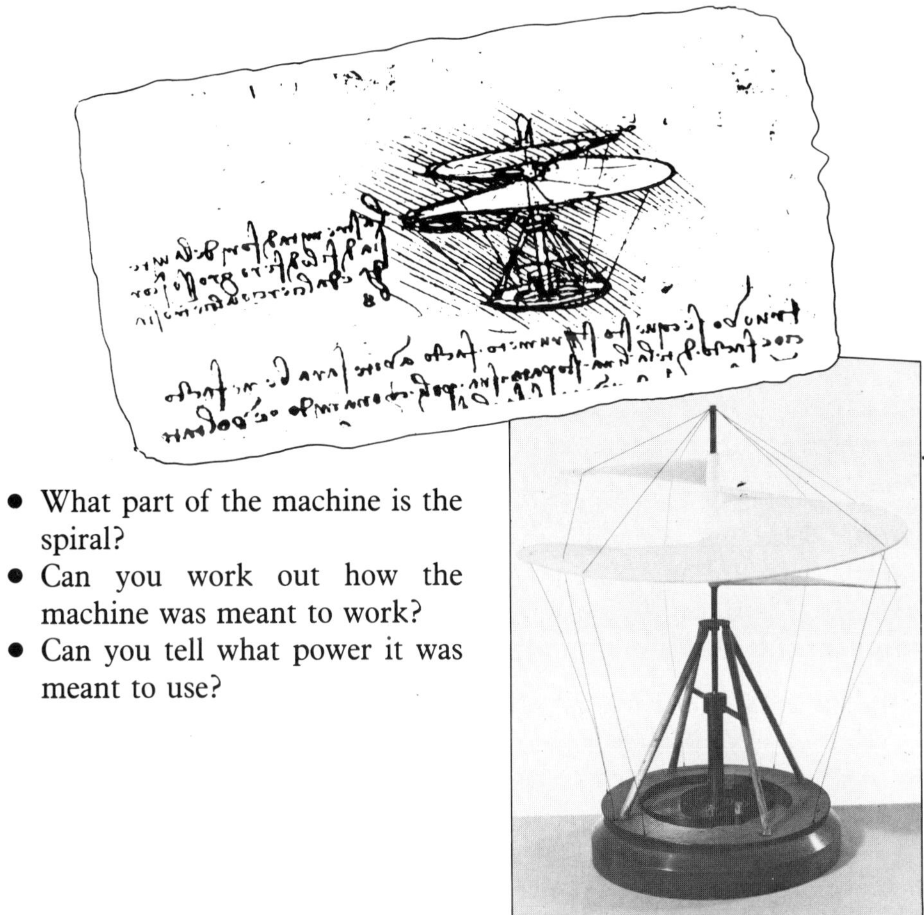

- What part of the machine is the spiral?
- Can you work out how the machine was meant to work?
- Can you tell what power it was meant to use?

The first really good idea for a helicopter came from George Cayley in 1843 who has already been mentioned on pages 9–11. This machine was known as Cayley's aerial carriage or the *convertiplane*. Besides a rudder and propellers for horizontal flight, it had rotors which could be used for vertical lift and then closed down to form circular biplane wings.

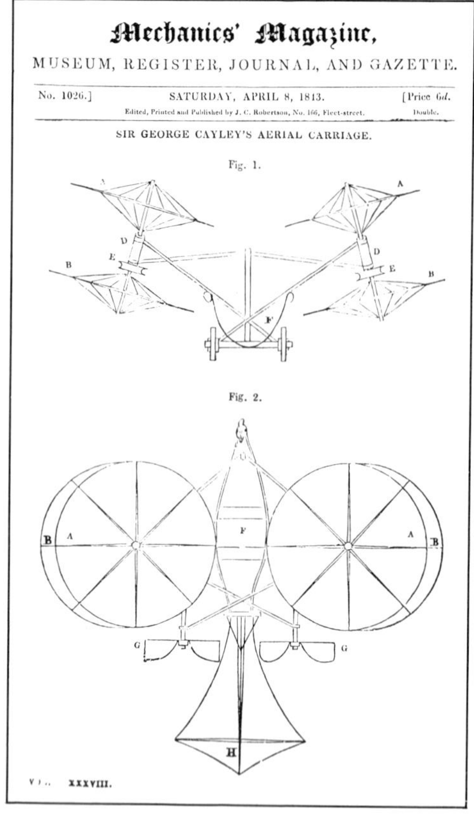

Mechanics' Magazine,

MUSEUM, REGISTER, JOURNAL, AND GAZETTE.

No. 1026.] SATURDAY, APRIL 8, 1813. [Price 6*d*.

Edited, Printed and Published by J. C. Robertson, No. 166, Fleet-street. Double.

SIR GEORGE CAYLEY'S AERIAL CARRIAGE.

Fig. 1.

Fig. 2.

XXXVIII.

As he had done with his ideas on gliders (see page 10), Cayley wrote about his ideas in the *Mechanics Magazine*. Look at the diagrams of the convertiplane on the front page of the magazine.

Here is a model which has been made of Cayley's aerial carriage.

- Why was it called a convertiplane? (Look up the word convertible in your dictionary.)
- Pick out the gondola two pusher propellers rotary wings tailplane and rudder undercarriage.

Helicopters are much more difficult to design than aeroplanes. The Spaniard Juan de la Cierva designed a machine which was a mixture of aeroplane and helicopter, called an *autogyro*. If an aeroplane suddenly loses speed, it *stalls* or begins to plunge downwards. De la Cierva worked out a way of preventing this. His machine had a rotor.

When the airspeed was high, the rotor acted like a fixed wing and kept the machine flying. When the airspeed dropped, and the machine began to fall, the moving air turned the rotor and gave enough lift to allow the machine to come down slowly. The rotor design was quickly improved and the autogyro was just one step away from today's helicopter.

When the rotors of a helicopter are powered to turn in one direction, this has the effect of causing the machine itself to turn in the opposite direction. Cayley and others had solved this problem by having two sets of rotors moving in opposite directions. Igor Sikorsky used a different idea and the first modern helicopter was made.

- Can you see what Sikorsky used instead of two large rotors going in different directions?
- Why was this machine tethered to the ground?
- What sorts of jobs do helicopters do today? What can helicopters do that most aeroplanes cannot?

Sikorsky at the controls of his helicopter on its first attempted flight

Flight into space

Once man had discovered means of flying across oceans and continents, attempts were made to fly into space and to seek out the moon and different planets.

As you have seen, flight records were usually set by individuals. The purpose was to be first and perhaps to win a large money prize. The competition for records in space travel, however, is between countries not individual people.

Why is this? Think about the money it takes to build a space-ship. Who are the main competitor countries involved in space travel today?

Yuri Gagarin

By the 1960s both the Russians and Americans had put satellites into space but they were unmanned. It was on Wednesday, 12 April 1961, that the Russian, Yuri Gagarin, became the first spaceman.

Here is the report from the *Daily Telegraph*, 13 April 1961. You will need a dictionary.

RUSSIAN SPACE MAN SAFELY BACK

Sky 'very, very dark' and World 'blue'

MAJOR YURI ALEXEYEVITCH GAGARIN, 27, dubbed "the Columbus of interplanetary space" by Moscow radio, yesterday won for Russia the race to make the first manned space flight. His 4½ ton space ship completed an orbit of the earth in 89.1 minutes, at a height of up to 190 miles, landing safely at the chosen place.

The rocket carrying the space ship Vostok (East) was launched at 9.07 a.m. Moscow time (7.07 British Summer Time). Major Gagarin, wearing a space suit and strapped to a couch, could do nothing to control his flight though he had a two-way wireless to operate and instruments to read.

Television enabled scientists to watch Major Gagarin during the flight, while instruments transmitted information about his physical reactions. Braking rockets to bring the ship back to earth were fired 90 minutes after the launching and at 8.55 a.m. BST the Major was back on Russian soil.

- What does 'the Columbus of interplanetary space' mean?
- How long did the flight take?
- What do you think were the purposes of the flight?

Everybody was impressed with the Russian achievement, but for some it posed problems.

Read this extract from the *Daily Telegraph*, 13 April 1961.

"SOME TIME" FOR U.S. TO CATCH UP

PRESIDENT KENNEDY tonight described Russia's manned space flight as "a most impressive scientific achievement." It would be "some time" before the United States caught up with Russia in space achievements.

America has put up 40 satellites to Russia's 16. She can reasonably claim to have covered more of the spectrum of scientific research and to have made more progress in putting satellites to immediately practical uses. Development of satellites for world communications, weather forecasting and military reconnaissance is well advanced.

But Russia's bigger rockets and satellites give her a lead in what will be a long contest to assert authority in space. Establishment of a manned space platform, or the landing of men on the moon, would give America good reason for serious alarm.

- What are space satellites used for?
- What do you think are the purposes of countries who enter the 'space-race'?

Valentina Tereshkova

Russia also sent the first woman, Valentina Tereshkova, into space.

Read these two newspaper extracts from 17 June 1963 carefully and look at the photographs which were printed with them. Both are describing the same event. The first is from the *Daily Mail* and the second is from *The Times*.

Date in Space

VALYA and Valery yesterday kept the world's first date in space.

Valentina Tereshkova, 26—Mr. Kruschev called her Valya—and family man Valery Bykovsky, 28, are circling the earth only 12 seconds apart.

Millions of Russians watching television saw Valya, the world's first space-woman, smile and talk happily as she sped towards the strangest-yet boy-meets-girl encounter.

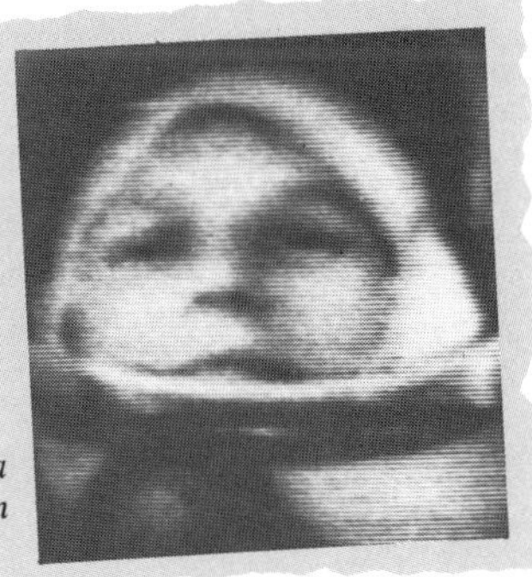

First spacewoman Valentina Tereshkova ... TV picture from space

RUSSIA SENDS WOMAN INTO SPACE

JOINT FLIGHT PROGRAMME WITH COL. BYKOVSKY

The first woman cosmonaut, Miss Valentina Tereshkova, today began a joint flight programme with Lieutenant-Colonel Bykovsky, the fifth Russian space man. As their spaceships orbited close together, observers thought it possible that they would attempt a rendezvous closer than the four miles of the Russians Andrian Nikolayev and Pavel Popovich.

"Seagull"—Miss Tereshkova's call-sign—was sent up at 12.30 p.m. (0930 G.M.T.) to join "Hawk", the call-sign of Colonel Bykovsky, who was launched two days ago.

According to official figures, the space pair are orbiting the earth with only 14½ seconds difference in their timing—with Miss Tereshkova taking the longer, 88.3 minutes.

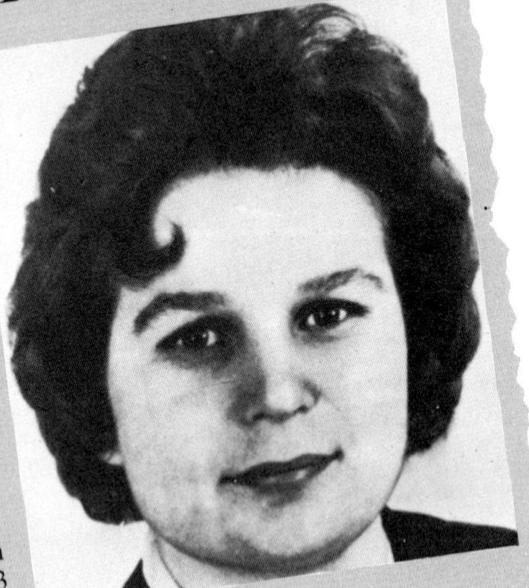

Valentina Tereshkova

- *The Daily Mail* says that the two Russians were keeping a date. What does this mean?
- Both extracts say how many seconds apart the cosmonauts are. Do they agree? There is one phrase in *The Times* extract which might make you think that this paper gives the right time. What is the phrase?
- Would you say that both extracts give exactly the same information? Which one gives most? Do not forget the pictures.

The Moonlanding

After the spaceflights of Gagarin and Tereshkova the Americans made great efforts in space. They took the lead in the space race when on Sunday, 20 July 1969, a manned American spacecraft landed on the moon.

This is the front page of the *Daily Mail* the next day.

FIRST OF ALL...

Daily Mail

NO. 22,772

MONDAY, JULY 21, 1969

At the last moment Armstrong grabs the controls to hop over 'football-field crater'

MAN ON THE MOON

CHEERS from Armstrong's parents as they hear of the landing at their home in Wapakoneta, Ohio. Armstrong's wife Jan cried out: 'Good! Good! Good!' when she heard the news.—Full story: Page TWO.

From ANGUS MACPHERSON, Houston, Sunday

THEY'RE on the Moon! While the world held its breath Neil Armstrong and Edwin Aldrin touched down today dead on time in their landing craft Eagle and began preparing for man's first fantastic steps on another planet.

As they touched down at 9.17 and 40sec. BST tonight Armstrong revealed a last-moment hitch that might have meant disaster.

He had to take control of the Eagle landing craft back from the computer at the very last stage. 'The auto-targeting was taking us right into a football-field-sized crater,' he told Houston ground control.

'It required firing manually over the rock field to find a reasonably good area.' Mission control at Houston reassured him: 'It was beautiful from here.'

ARMSTRONG: 'The rocks are grey'

- What was the name of the landing craft?
- What did Armstrong do to avoid a last-minute disaster?
- Why was the newspaper report from Houston, Texas?

The moonlanding was different from the other 'firsts' described in this book because millions of people all around the world were able to watch the event on television 'live', as it happened. The moonlanding was planned in advance and so television companies could include it in their programmes. On the following page is the cover of the *TV Times* for the week of the moonlanding.

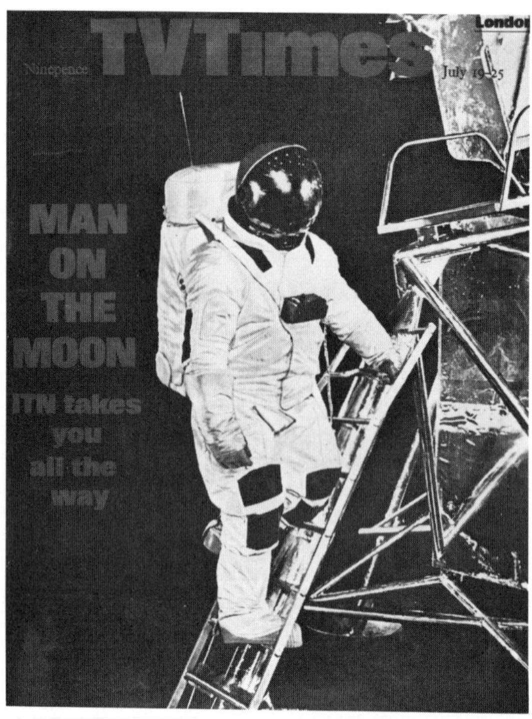

Due to television, people could see the evidence of man walking on the moon with their own eyes and did not have to rely on newspaper reports after the event. Together with the pictures, the world was able to hear the live conversations between the astronauts and their controllers at the command centre at Houston. Here is a *transcription* of the conversation which took place just before the lunar module landed.

Control:	Eagle looking great. You're go.
Eagle:	220ft. Coming down nicely. 75ft., looking good ... 30ft., kicking up some dust ... just moving to the right a little ... contact light ... okay. Engine stopped ... defuel on the descent [engine] ... engine auto over. Out ... engine arm off ... [inaudible]. Is in.
Control:	Roger, we copy. You're down, Eagle.
Eagle:	Tranquillity base here. The Eagle has landed.

What is 'live' television? When it is not live, what has happened? Is there any way in which events shown on live TV can be *edited* or changed? News broadcasts on television often contain short films of important events which have been filmed some time before. The television producers have chosen which parts to show and also choose the *commentary*, or explanation to go with the pictures.

Do you think television is a good or bad source of evidence?

Space Shuttle

Space ships and rockets are very expensive and soon people, and governments, wanted a cheaper way to fly into space. The main problem had been that once a rocket had been used, it could not be used a second time. In America, the space scientists developed a space ship which could be used over and over again, like an aeroplane. They called the spacecraft, the *space shuttle*. Why 'shuttle'?

The first one was launched in April 1981 and this is how the *Daily Mirror* reported it.

OUT OF THIS WORLD

THEY'RE back! And after fifty-four hours in orbit, America's astronauts brought their Space shuttle down to a landing smooth enough to make an airline captain green with envy.

Millions of TV viewers round the world watched enthralled as the 75-ton Columbia touched down only nine seconds late after circling the earth thirty-six times...

It began 8,000 miles out when Young and his co-pilot, Bob Crippen, fired the twin motors to take the spacecraft out of its orbit and drop it back into the Earth's atmosphere.

"It's flying like a champ," Crippen reported as the re-entry friction began to slow the craft from 17,500 mph to a more manageable 700 mph for the final left-hand circuit and approach.

"Beautiful, beautiful," murmured controller Joe Allen at the base as the gentle touchdown kicked up a long plume of dust.

This is how the *Daily Mail* illustrated the end of the voyage.

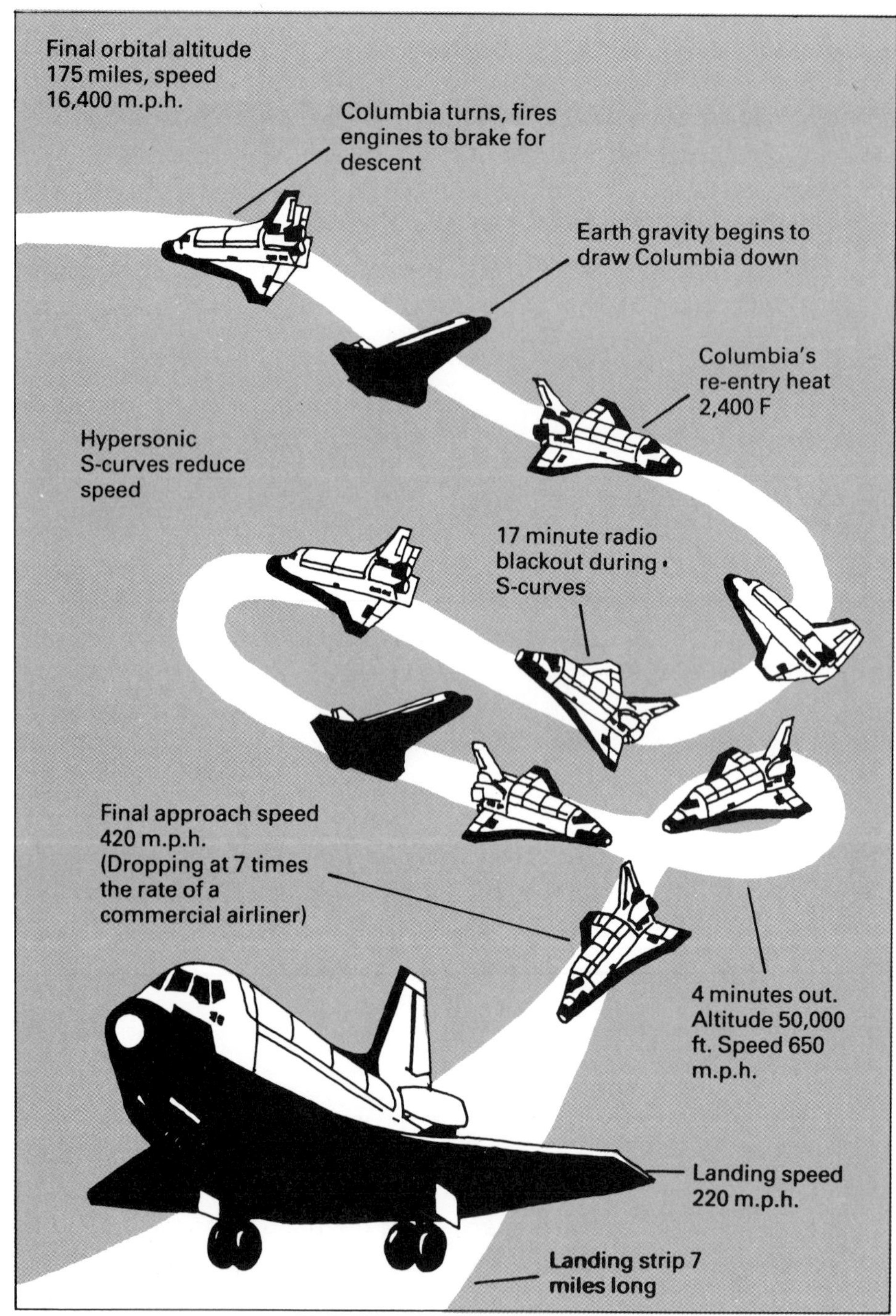

Do you think it is very different from the *Daily Mirror* report. Which do you think is clearer and more accurate?

The future?

In future spacecraft will be used to travel further than man has ever been. Spacemen may not go beyond the moon this century but unmanned spacecraft, called *probes*, will be used to increase our knowledge of the solar system and beyond.

Interplanetary travel is difficult and these journeys may last for months or even years. Travel beyond our solar system involves such huge distances that there are many problems.

- Make a list of problems for travellers journeying over vast distances to other star systems.

In 1972 the space probe, *Pioneer 10*, was launched. It will be the first man-made object to leave our Solar System. It carries this message.

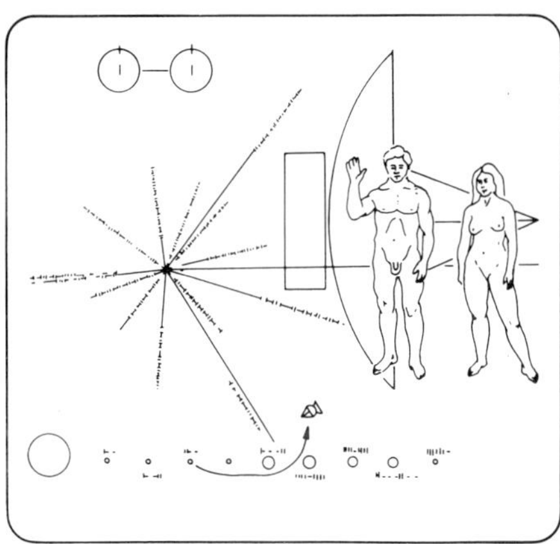

- Can you work out what any of it might mean?
- Why are there no words?
- Who do you think might read it?
- Design a message of your own telling alien space beings something about yourself. Do not use any words.

Time travel

In this chapter we have been looking at man's conquest of distance. Some travellers seek to conquer time as well as distance. Some think transport in the future might link the two more closely. This is because stars and planets outside our solar system are hundreds and thousands of *light years* away. Find out what a light year is. Journeys to these places would therefore take thousands of years. To overcome this, either a new spacecraft will have to be invented which travels huge distances in seconds, or time will have to be conquered.

What do you think will happen to space travel in the future?

INDEX

ACKNOWLEDGEMENTS

The author and publishers would like to thank the following for permission to reproduce material:

Ancient Art and Architecture Collection **p 5**; Associated Press **pp 57, 58**; Aviation Photographs International **cover** (top); Constance Babington Smith **p 32**; Barnabys Picture Library **p 34**; BBC Hulton Picture Library **pp 33, 36, 37**; British Library Newspaper Library **pp 24, 59, 60, 62**; British Museum **p 4** (× 2); Commonwealth War Graves Commission **p 43**; *Daily Mail* **pp 15/16, 28, 38, 57, 59, 62**; *Daily Mirror* **pp 14, 24, 25, 29, 36, 38, 40, 61**; *Daily Telegraph* **pp 56, 57**; *East Anglian Daily Times* **pp 22/23**; East Yorkshire Borough Council **pp 30/31**; Mary Evans Picture Library **p 8** (bottom); Carey Fisher **p 35**; J F P Galvin **cover** (background); Greater London History Library **p 51** (top); Historical Aviation Service **p 49**; Imperial War Museum **pp 19** (× 2), **20, 22** (× 2), **42, 44**; Library of Congress, Washington **p 12**; Adrian Meredith Photography **pp 47** (bottom × 2), **51** (bottom); *Radio Times* **p 60**; Royal Aeronautical Society **pp 54** (top), 55; Royal Air Force Museum **pp 26, 45** (× 6), **46** (× 4), **47** (top × 6); Science Museum **pp 6** (× 2), **7, 8** (top), **10, 11, 13, 27, 53** (× 2), **54** (bottom); Stanley Gibbons Ltd **p 46**; Sutton Libraries and Arts Services **p 50**; *The Times* **p 15, 28, 58**; Topham Picture Library **p 28**.

Designed by Julian Smith